D0876139

COMICS
JOURNAL

WRITTEN & ILLUSTRATED BY
BRUCE
WALDMAN

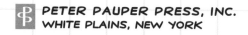

PETER PAUPER PRESS, INC.
WHITE PLAINS, NEW YORK

PETER PAUPER PRESS
FINE BOOKS AND GIFTS SINCE 1928

OUR STORY

In 1928, at the age of twenty-two, our hero Peter Beilenson began printing books on a small press in the basement of his parents' home in Larchmont, New York. Peter—and later, his sidekick, Edna—sought to create fine books that sold at "prices even a pauper could afford."

Today, still family owned and operated, Peter Pauper Press continues to honor our founders' legacy—and our customers' expectations—of beauty, quality, and value.

Designed by Heather Zschock
Illustrations © 2016 Bruce Waldman

Copyright © 2016 Peter Pauper Press, Inc.
202 Mamaroneck Avenue
White Plains, New York 10601 USA

All rights reserved
ISBN 978-1-4413-2168-8
Printed in China

7 6 5 4 3 2 1

Visit us at www.peterpauper.com

INTRODUCTION

In essence, comic books and graphic novels are pictures arranged in a sequence to tell a story. They use the visual language of art to communicate ideas and impressions with an immediacy not possible through words alone. The comics I like best combine the virtues of visual and verbal storytelling to create a many-layered, uniquely compelling reading experience.

Comics and graphic novels have fans of all ages, all around the world. This is great, because it means you can use the format to tell all kinds of stories, from spacefaring adventures to haunting memoirs to superhero epics to adaptations of classic books to slice-of-life tales for kids. In this book you'll find guidance for starting to create your own comics, whatever story you want to tell.

The pages ahead cover the fundamentals of visual storytelling, from basic **drawing reference** to advice for conceptualizing your comics. Read through, then plan your panels in words and sketches in the **layout pages** section. When you're ready, draw up to 66 pages of **final comics** in the blue-lined pages ruled with reference points along the borders. The blue guidelines on the final and layout pages are non-reproductive and won't show up on copies, so you can create clean prints when your comic is ready to be seen.

The advice in the **drawing reference** section is just that. There are no hard and fast rules for making comics, and exploring the medium's possibilities is part of the fun. Go ahead and experiment. Then, share your work with the world.

HOW TO USE THIS COMICS JOURNAL

Once you have an idea of the story you'd like to tell, begin planning it out in the **layout pages**.

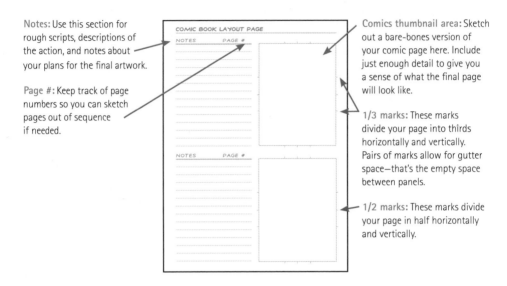

Notes: Use this section for rough scripts, descriptions of the action, and notes about your plans for the final artwork.

Page #: Keep track of page numbers so you can sketch pages out of sequence if needed.

Comics thumbnail area: Sketch out a bare-bones version of your comic page here. Include just enough detail to give you a sense of what the final page will look like.

1/3 marks: These marks divide your page into thirds horizontally and vertically. Pairs of marks allow for gutter space—that's the empty space between panels.

1/2 marks: These marks divide your page in half horizontally and vertically.

If you can't decide how best to show something, sketch several layout thumbnails and choose the best of them. For tips on panel and page composition, see pages 24 to 25.

When you like your layout pages and are ready to create your finished comic, use the **final art pages**.

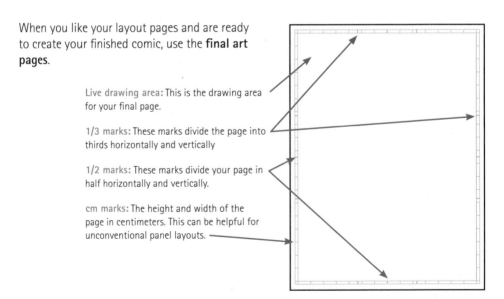

Live drawing area: This is the drawing area for your final page.

1/3 marks: These marks divide the page into thirds horizontally and vertically

1/2 marks: These marks divide your page in half horizontally and vertically.

cm marks: The height and width of the page in centimeters. This can be helpful for unconventional panel layouts.

SUGGESTED MATERIALS

All you really need to get started making comics is a pencil, and unless you prefer to create finished graphite drawings, a pen. However, many people like to work with a selection of the following:

DRAWING TOOLS:

- **Pencils with both hard and soft leads.** Soft leads draw darker lines.

- **Erasable colored pencil in non-photo blue.** Mechanical pencil lead is also available in this color.

- **A plastic eraser and a kneaded eraser.** Plastic erasers are very effective, and kneaded erasers can be used to gently lift pencil off the surface of the paper without damage.

- **A ruler and/or T-square.** A ruler will help you achieve straight lines in panel borders and elsewhere. A T-square makes it easy to draw perfectly vertical or horizontal lines—just align the T bar with the side of the page perpendicular to the line you want to draw.

- **Drafting triangles, French curves, a compass, and/or a circle template.** These aren't necessary, but can help if you want to draw precise angles, curves, and circles.

INKING TOOLS:

- **Permanent, waterproof fine line pens.** These are also known as technical pens, have metal or fiber tips, and yield a line of very even width. It's best to get a range of tip sizes.

- **Fountain pens or dip pens.** These can be more expressive than technical pens, with line width that varies depending on pressure. They can take some getting used to, but are well worth it. A crow quill pen is best for fine linework.

- **A black ink brush pen, or small round brush.** A brush is the most dynamic inking tool and in many ways also the most challenging. Pre-loaded felt or bristle-tip brush pens are convenient, though traditional paintbrushes dipped in ink can offer more versatility.

- **Black ink.** Permanent, waterproof India ink is best for inking. Ink can be diluted with water to produce shades of grey. Note: Be careful to clean any tools you use with ink before it dries.

NOTE: You can also use markers and watercolor paint, among other media, to shade and color your comics. If you use heavy or wet materials such as markers, paint, or water-diluted ink in this book, you'll want to place a protective sheet beneath your page to preserve the pages behind it.

DRAWING REFERENCE

From composition to the proportions of the human figure, the knowledge that can help you create a strong drawing will also prove invaluable in making comics. Ahead are some drawing fundamentals to keep in mind, and the particular ways they apply to comics.

ONE-POINT PERSPECTIVE

Perspective is a way of simplifying the complex things our brains intuitively understand about depth, in order to draw 3D objects on a 2D surface. Illustrators commonly use **one-point**, **two-point**, and **three-point** perspective, as well as combinations of all three.

One-point perspective is easy. In the drawing below, the ground and the sky meet at the **horizon line**. We often can't see the horizon in real life. Other things—buildings and trees, for example—are in the way. But we know it's there and it informs how we see everything around us. **In drawing, it is our eye-level line. Your reader sees the scene from same height as the horizon line.**

Horizon Line

Vanishing Point

A **vanishing point**—the place in the distance where diagonal lines, such as those of the train tracks, seem to come together—is located on the horizon line. One-point perspective gets its name from the fact that it has **one vanishing point.**

> **TIP:** Think of yourself like the director of a movie framing a shot. You can make your reader look at the scene you're drawing from any angle you want. Create different moods by placing the horizon line and vanishing point in different places.

ONE-POINT PERSPECTIVE IN BUILDINGS AND CITIES

In the two drawings here, perspective lines are integrated like a matrix underneath the cityscapes. They converge on the single vanishing point, whether they are above or below the horizon line. In addition to determining things like the angle of the buildings' roofs, they determine the size of objects such as near and far cars on the road.

TIP: It's helpful to use a ruler or other straightedge for perspective drawings, especially of buildings. But for quick sketches, it may be simpler to do without a ruler.

ONE-POINT PERSPECTIVE IN LANDSCAPES

Irregularly-shaped and -sized objects in nature won't conform precisely to perspective lines, but you can still use perspective as an underlying framework for your landscapes. Perspective lines can dictate the sizes of natural objects like the trees in this drawing as they get farther away.

DRAWING FIGURES WITH ONE-POINT PERSPECTIVE

To help keep a character in proportion, draw her or him, then draw perspective lines from head and feet to the vanishing point on the horizon line. This way, you will know what a character's height should be if you move him or her backward in your scene. Remember that the horizon line is your reader's eye level. In fact, one way to catch your reader's eye is to position characters so that their eyes are looking at your reader from on the horizon line.

TWO-POINT PERSPECTIVE

Use two-point perspective when you intend for your reader to face the **corner** of something, such as a building. Imagine standing on a street corner, looking at the corner of the opposite block. The buildings on the left side of the corner seem to "shrink" toward the left horizon line; the buildings on the right are reduced in size toward the right. To depict this, **you need two vanishing points, one to the left side of the horizon line and one to the right**. Note that vertical lines in two-point perspective are parallel.

As with one-point perspective, you can use two-point perspective to draw images from a variety of angles. This includes scenes with flying or hovering objects, such as the floating block in the drawing on the left.

CROWDS IN PERSPECTIVE

To give a feeling of depth, this illustration uses two-point perspective to determine the heights of the distant figures. Two vanishing points sit off to the sides, and the man in the cap—the focal point of the image—is the "corner." The heights of the two men behind him correspond roughly to perspective guidelines.

VANISHING OFF THE PAGE

You might find it helpful to place **one or both vanishing points outside your page or panel**. Doing so will soften the angles in your image.

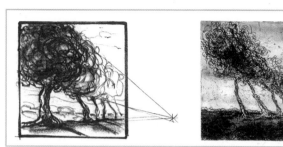

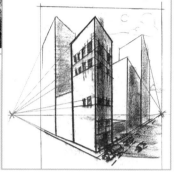

TIP: When vanishing points are far from the subject of your drawing, using a straightedge is key! It's harder to eyeball the angle of perspective lines at greater distances, and sketched lines may "wander." Rely on your straightedge instead.

THREE-POINT PERSPECTIVE

Three-point perspective adds a third vanishing point above or below the horizon line. It will allow you to create unusual and dramatic compositions. If you'd like to depict the viewpoint of someone gazing up at a tall building, or looking down from a helicopter, three-point perspective is your best bet. In essence, it lets you draw objects vanishing in three different directions.

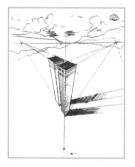

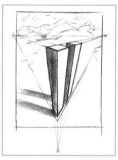

Three-point perspective can be a great tool for conveying size. The drawing on the left uses three-point perspective to indirectly convey the scale of the landscape. The buildings appear large as they recede, but they also look tiny compared to the mountains.

DRAWING PEOPLE

FACES

All human faces are unique, but most have the same structure.

From the front, the **head** is egg-shaped. Start with lines that divide the head in half horizontally and vertically.

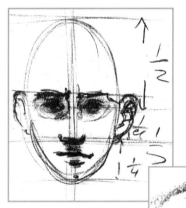

Place the **eyes** so that their pupils are on the horizontal halfway line. There should be an eye-length between the eyes, and an eye-length between each eye and the outside edge of the face. In other words, the face is about five eye-lengths across. When placing the eyebrow and shading around the eye, note that the eyeball is much smaller than the eye socket, as it has to fit inside it like a golf ball in a hole. The eye socket is recessed and will therefore be shadowed in most lighting.

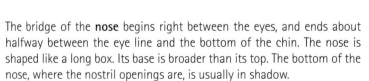

The bridge of the **nose** begins right between the eyes, and ends about halfway between the eye line and the bottom of the chin. The nose is shaped like a long box. Its base is broader than its top. The bottom of the nose, where the nostril openings are, is usually in shadow.

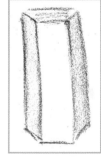

The **mouth** sits halfway between the bottom of the nose and the bottom of the chin. Its corners often line up with the center of each eye. The upper lip tends to form a loose "M" shape. It's generally thinner and more shadowed than the lower lip. The lower lip is fuller, with the deepest shadow right beneath the center of it.

The top of the average **ear** is level with the eyebrow, and the bottom is level with the bottom of the nose.

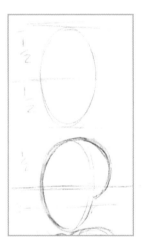

From the side, begin the **head** with two shapes: an egg shape and a ball representing the back of the skull. The bottom of the ball meets the egg shape about halfway between the eye line and the bottom of the nose. The egg shape indents on the eye line, representing the bridge of the nose. **Eyes** look almost triangular from the side, because you are seeing half of the eye's full almond shape. Leave space between the eye and the outer contour of the face. The end of the **nostril** aligns approximately with the front of the eye socket, and the end of the mouth aligns approximately with the center of the eye socket. There is about a socket-length between the end of the eye socket and the **ear**. The **chin** can vary, but should align roughly with the front of the eye socket.

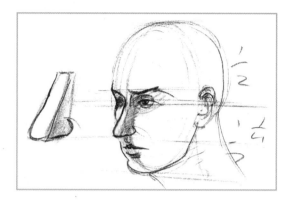

Like profile views, **three-quarter views** begin with an egg shape for the face and a ball for the back of the head. Start with the egg and the horizontal guidelines, then add a guideline for the **center of the face**. This line should follow the curve of the face's outer contour. It **determines the angle of the head.**

The closer the center line is to the middle of the egg shape, the more you see of the side of the face that's farther from you, and the less you see of the back of the head. (And vice versa: The closer the center line is to the outer contour of the face, the less you see of the face's far side, and the more you see of the back of the head.)

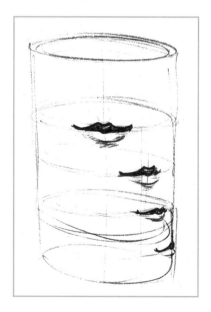

To understand how features turn in space, think of the head as a cylinder. On the cylinder to the left, as the mouths rotate away, the nearer side of the mouth becomes very slightly shortened. The far side of the mouth, however, dramatically shortens, eventually disappearing from view altogether.

Masculine and feminine features don't differ as much as you might think. To make a character lean one way or the other, pay attention to the width of the shoulders and the neck. Women tend to have narrower, more sloping shoulders, and men often have thicker necks with more prominent Adam's apples.

When drawing **hair**, keep in mind the shape of the head beneath it. Instead of trying to draw every strand, use lines that suggest the texture of the hair (e.g., straight, curly) to depict the overall shape of the hair.

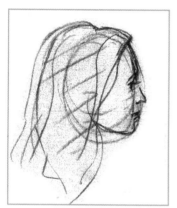 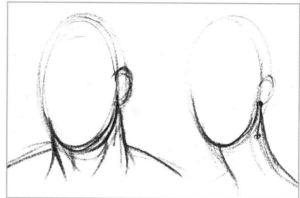

EXPRESSIONS

A lot about a person's mood can be conveyed through the **language of eyebrows**. Picture a triangle superimposed over the character's face, with one tip in the center of the face. Point the triangle down for anger and other antagonistic emotions. Point it up for sadness, happiness, and surprise. The taller the triangle, the more extreme the emotion. Complex emotions such as bewilderment, confusion, irritation, disappointment, and suspicion can be expressed by subtle changes in the brows, eyes, and mouth.

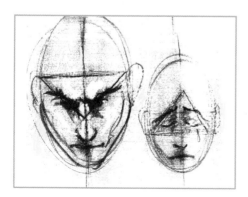 

THE HUMAN FIGURE

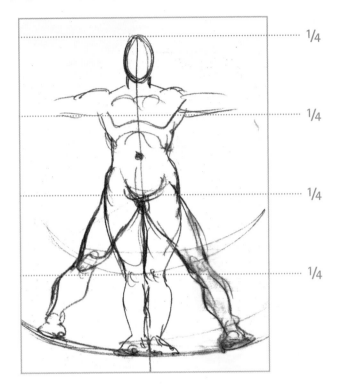

The **standing human figure** is about six and a half to eight heads tall, with seven heads being the average. The center of the pelvic girdle (the hips) is halfway between the top of the head and the bottom of the feet. Think of the figure's height as divided into four quarters:

1. From the bottom of the foot to the kneecap is ¼ of the figure's height.

2. From the kneecap to the center of the hips is another ¼.

3. From the hips to the top of the ribcage is the next ¼.

4. From the top of the ribcage to the top of the head is the final ¼.

THE SPINE AND THE LINE OF ACTION

It's often helpful to begin with a straight or curved line showing the angle of the person's **spine**, and arrange the figure's structure around this line. Starting with the spine's shape will make the final pose feel more physically plausible and dynamic.

You may also want to note where the bottoms of the character's **feet** will be, and/or any other **points of contact** between them and their environment. (If they're punching a wall, for example, pencil a quick mark where their knuckles meet the wall.) Integrating these points of contact into your drawing from the start will make your character feel like they're really part of the scene.

Breaking a pose down into simple lines and geometric shapes at the beginning will help you figure out how the human body turns in space. Rather than trying to draw every contour from the start, sketch loose suggestions of the figure's shape. Arms and legs are roughly tubular, so draw them first as **cylinders** for a sense of how they relate to the rest of the body, as well as its surroundings. Try using a large circle for the pelvis; smaller circles for joints; an oval for the torso; and an oval for the head.

The palm is a five-sided shape, like an uneven pentagon. From it extend the four fingers. For most of us, the middle finger is the longest. The index and ring fingers to either side are slightly shorter, and the pinky is shorter still. Each finger has a **knuckle and two joints**. Use curved guidelines to help you place the two joints above the knuckle on each finger.

The **thumb** consists of a knuckle and one joint. It extends from a pad of muscle that makes up one "corner" of the palm.

A **closed fist** forms a boxy shape. Use a block as a general guideline for the fist, then delineate the individual fingers and thumb.

The fingers of a hand in action are often partially bent, meaning that you can see only one or two knuckles, and the fingers appear *foreshortened* (See page 18).

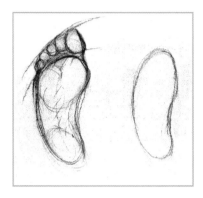

From the bottom, a foot is shaped a little like a kidney bean. If you're drawing a bare foot, it may help to envision it as a slipper or shoe at first.

From the front, feet look triangular. The foot gets taller and tapers as it nears the ankle, and the ankle bones stick out just above the foot. Start by drawing toes as a single long block.

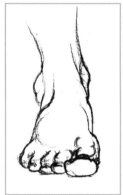

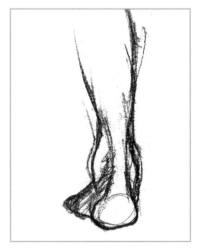

From the back, the **heel** is shaped like a squat oval or a clementine fruit. It tapers sharply into the Achilles tendon, beyond which the ankle bones are visible. One or both sides of the front of the foot may be visible in the form of low triangular wedges.

FORESHORTENING

Foreshortening is how you represent that one part of a character's body is closer to the reader than another—when their outstretched hand reaches into the foreground of the panel, for example, or when you depict someone from a low angle and their feet are much closer to the viewer than their head. It can be subtle or dramatic. Foreshortening part or all of a person's body is basically drawing it in perspective, and you can approach it similarly to how you would a landscape in perspective, **using regular lines and shapes as guides for irregular lines and shapes**.

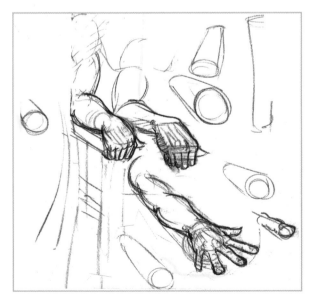

When drawing foreshortened limbs, start with tubes or cylinders. It's hard to envision the complicated curvature of an arm receding in space, but the way a simple cylinder narrows as it gets farther away is easier.

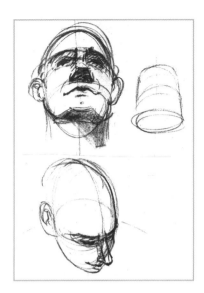

To draw non-tubular parts of the body in perspective, begin by envisioning them inside a cylinder. Use the cylinder to guide the size and placement of features, as for a turning head in ¾ view (see page 12). When part of a body tilts, the features that are farther away from the viewer become compressed. The features that are closer appear larger. At extreme angles, some features obscure others from view.

Varying the angle from which you depict characters dramatically impacts the mood of a panel. Showing characters from below can make them feel imposing; from above, they look small and vulnerable, or like they are shouldering a great responsibility. Featuring hands in the extreme foreground emphasizes their gesture—accusatory pointing, or hands raised in surrender.

LIGHT, SHADOW, AND DIMENSION

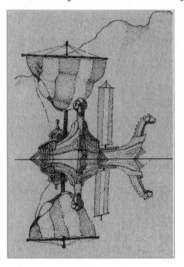

You can use linework to make things come forward and recede in space. **Darker, thicker lines look closer to the viewer; lighter, finer lines look farther away.** If you're coloring or shading your comic, **sharper contrast and more intense colors look closer to the viewer; softer contrast and more muted colors look farther away.**

CHARACTERS

Your comic will be both easier to follow and more compelling if your characters are visually distinct. Research is the surest path—look at photos, artwork, and people in real life who resemble your vision for the character in some way. Note not only their physical characteristics but how they carry themselves, gestures that seem particular to them, and how they dress. If possible, surround yourself with research images when you sit down to draw. Try to make your characters instantly recognizable, and difficult to confuse with one another.

TIP: It's crucial to keep your character looking **consistent from panel to panel**. Many artists therefore create a "style guide" for each character, outlining their distinguishing features so they don't get altered or forgotten. This can be meticulously detailed or consist simply of a few sketches of your character, displaying their features from different views.

CREATURES AND MONSTERS

When designing creatures and monsters, it's important to first consider your creature's role in the story. Is it an antagonist? If so, is it intelligent and scheming, angry, or simply hungry? Is it an ally, the protagonist, or neutral? Do you want to scare the reader or move them to compassion?

Start by researching the real-life animals on which you want to base your creature. Choose those with features suited to the environment your creature will inhabit, or just those you like the look of. Pick aspects of different animals—a bear's big shoulders, a hawk's hooked beak—and exaggerate them. Sketch several configurations before you settle on one.

You have a choice between depicting animal features as they appear in life or mapping aspects of human expression onto them (see page 13). The former is more realistic, and will make your creatures feel more alien and "other" to the reader. The latter can be tricky, but will let you portray a wider range of recognizable expressions on the creature's face, and make your creature more sympathetic to the reader. You might, for example, allow a dragon's lizard-like brow ridges to furrow like eyebrows in anger or surprise; or move an animal's eyes from the sides of its head to the front, so it can assume more humanlike facial expressions. Making an animal's face more human can render it cartoonish or uncanny, though, so take care if that isn't your aim.

DEPICTING MOTION

Techniques for creating a sense of motion vary. A time-honored one is motion lines or "speed lines"—a series of close, fine lines across the image in the direction of the movement, intended to mimic the blur of motion. You can also imitate motion blur by simply blurring parts of the image. Drawing a character's face in sharp relief and their arcing fist as a loose, streaky-edged shape indicates that the fist is in motion.

Little cues signal and accentuate movement. When someone lunges forward, their hair and clothing blow backward a little. Their hat might get knocked askew. They might fling an arm out to break their fall.

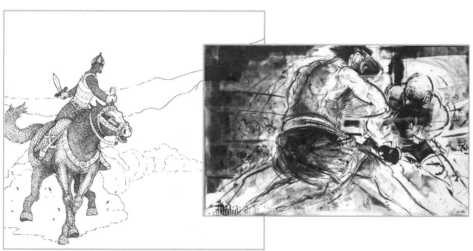

TIP: A good way to make motion feel real in your comics is to move when you draw them. Keep your arm loose and draw gesturally. The movement will come through in your work.

COMPOSITION AND PANEL FLOW

Composition is the **arrangement of positive and negative space** (filled and empty space, respectively) in an image. It can make the difference between a vivid, striking image and a muddy, confusing one.

When you draw comics, consider both the composition of each individual panel and the composition of the whole page. Individually, each panel should clearly convey an action or dialogue exchange. Together, the panels should create a distinctive visual and emotional impression, and should guide the reader through reading the panels in order.

Whether you're working on the arrangement of one panel or a whole page, here are three general guidelines to keep in mind:

1. **Try not to place anything right in the center of the panel or page**. Your reader's eye will be drawn to the center, and can get "stuck" there instead of reading the page in the right order. Sticking something smack in the middle can also create a static, motionless composition. (There are exceptions to this—use your best judgment!)

2. Vary the **sizes, shapes, and spacing** of objects.

3. **Keep your compositions simple.** Even when you're depicting a complex and busy scene, establish clear overall areas of light and dark.

Most readers will read a page from left to right, and from top to bottom. Lay your page out accordingly, and try to "lead" your reader's eye to the next panel with the composition of your artwork.

THUMBNAILS AND LAYOUT SKETCHES

Before you start the final art for each page, experiment with different compositions using the layout pages in this book.

Don't get too bogged down in details when creating quick sketches, or thumbnail sketches. Render the sketch just enough to give an impression of the final art. It can help to think of drawing the final page as it would look from a distance—all you see are the **major shapes and areas of light and shadow.**

There are more layout templates than final art pages in this book. Often it will take a few tries before you settle on a layout that works. Try sketching a few versions of your page or panel contents on the same spread, so you can see them side by side, and choose the strongest one.

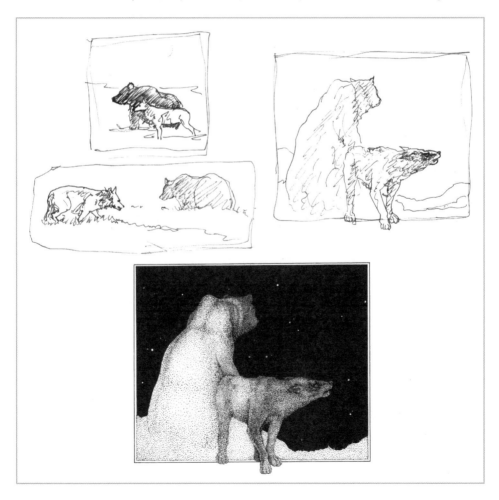

PUTTING IT ALL TOGETHER

Experiment with layouts until you find one you like. Consider light-dark balance, whether the eye flows naturally from panel to panel, and whether the action is clear. When you settle on a layout, section a final art page into panels and draw your comic lightly in pencil. Fine-tune the details in each panel.

Some artists like the soft look of a finished pencil page, and render their work to completion in (dark) pencil. Most, though, go over their pencil drawing with hard lines in ink. Experiment with inking tools to find the ones that work best with your style (see page 5).

Once you've completed a comic, scan or photocopy it to share it with the world. The non-photo blue templates won't reproduce in copies, so your work will show up crisp and clean.

LAYOUT PAGES

USE THESE PAGES TO CREATE PRELIMINARY SKETCHES FOR YOUR COMIC!

NOTES   PAGE #

THE TIRED, LONELY
ASTRONAUTS LAND
IN THEIR SPACESHIP.
THE LAND IS
DESOLATE AND
BLEAK, BUT THE HOT
SUN STILL BURNS
BRIGHTLY.

COMIC BOOK LAYOUT PAGE

NOTES   PAGE #

NOTES   PAGE #

NOTES   PAGE #

NOTES   PAGE #

COMIC BOOK LAYOUT PAGE

NOTES   PAGE #

NOTES   PAGE #

NOTES   PAGE #

NOTES   PAGE #

COMIC BOOK LAYOUT PAGE

NOTES   PAGE #

NOTES   PAGE #

NOTES   PAGE #

NOTES   PAGE #

COMIC BOOK LAYOUT PAGE

NOTES   PAGE #

NOTES   PAGE #

NOTES   PAGE #

NOTES   PAGE #

COMIC BOOK LAYOUT PAGE

NOTES   PAGE #

NOTES   PAGE #

TITLE:

NOTES   PAGE #

_____
_____
_____
_____
_____
_____
_____
_____
_____
_____
_____
_____
_____
_____
_____

NOTES   PAGE #

_____
_____
_____
_____
_____
_____
_____
_____
_____
_____
_____
_____
_____
_____
_____

COMIC BOOK LAYOUT PAGE

NOTES   PAGE #

NOTES   PAGE #

NOTES　　　　PAGE #

NOTES　　　　PAGE #

COMIC BOOK LAYOUT PAGE

NOTES   PAGE #

NOTES   PAGE #

TITLE:

NOTES   PAGE #

NOTES   PAGE #

COMIC BOOK LAYOUT PAGE

NOTES   PAGE #

NOTES   PAGE #

NOTES   PAGE #

NOTES   PAGE #

COMIC BOOK LAYOUT PAGE

NOTES   PAGE #

NOTES   PAGE #

NOTES PAGE #

NOTES PAGE #

COMIC BOOK LAYOUT PAGE

NOTES   PAGE #

NOTES   PAGE #

TITLE:

NOTES   PAGE #

NOTES   PAGE #

COMIC BOOK LAYOUT PAGE

NOTES   PAGE #

NOTES   PAGE #

NOTES   PAGE #

NOTES   PAGE #

COMIC BOOK LAYOUT PAGE

NOTES   PAGE #

NOTES   PAGE #

TITLE:

NOTES   PAGE #

_____
_____
_____
_____
_____
_____
_____
_____
_____
_____
_____
_____
_____

NOTES   PAGE #

_____
_____
_____
_____
_____
_____
_____
_____
_____
_____
_____
_____
_____

COMIC BOOK LAYOUT PAGE

NOTES   PAGE #

NOTES   PAGE #

TITLE:

NOTES   PAGE

NOTES   PAGE

COMIC BOOK LAYOUT PAGE

NOTES   PAGE #

NOTES   PAGE #

TITLE:

NOTES   PAGE #

_____

_____

_____

_____

_____

_____

_____

_____

_____

_____

_____

_____

_____

_____

NOTES   PAGE #

_____

_____

_____

_____

_____

_____

_____

_____

_____

_____

_____

_____

_____

_____

COMIC BOOK LAYOUT PAGE

NOTES   PAGE #

NOTES   PAGE #

NOTES   PAGE #

NOTES   PAGE #

COMIC BOOK LAYOUT PAGE

NOTES   PAGE #

NOTES   PAGE #

TITLE:

NOTES   PAGE #

_____

NOTES   PAGE #

_____

COMIC BOOK LAYOUT PAGE

NOTES   PAGE #

NOTES   PAGE #

TITLE:

NOTES   PAGE #

_____
_____
_____
_____
_____
_____
_____
_____
_____
_____
_____
_____
_____
_____
_____
_____

NOTES   PAGE #

_____
_____
_____
_____
_____
_____
_____
_____
_____
_____
_____
_____
_____
_____
_____
_____

COMIC BOOK LAYOUT PAGE

NOTES   PAGE #

NOTES   PAGE #

TITLE:

NOTES   PAGE #

_____
_____
_____
_____
_____
_____
_____
_____
_____
_____
_____
_____
_____

NOTES   PAGE #

_____
_____
_____
_____
_____
_____
_____
_____
_____
_____
_____
_____
_____

COMIC BOOK LAYOUT PAGE

NOTES   PAGE

NOTES   PAGE

NOTES   PAGE #

NOTES   PAGE #

COMIC BOOK LAYOUT PAGE

NOTES   PAGE #

NOTES   PAGE #

NOTES　　　　PAGE #

NOTES　　　　PAGE #

COMIC BOOK LAYOUT PAGE

NOTES   PAGE #

NOTES   PAGE #

NOTES   PAGE #

_____

NOTES   PAGE #

_____

COMIC BOOK LAYOUT PAGE

NOTES   PAGE #

NOTES   PAGE #

NOTES   PAGE #

NOTES   PAGE #

COMIC BOOK LAYOUT PAGE

NOTES   PAGE #

NOTES   PAGE #

NOTES   PAGE #

NOTES   PAGE #

COMIC BOOK LAYOUT PAGE

NOTES　　　　　PAGE #

NOTES　　　　　PAGE #

NOTES | PAGE #

NOTES | PAGE #

COMIC BOOK LAYOUT PAGE

NOTES   PAGE #

NOTES   PAGE #

NOTES PAGE #

NOTES PAGE #

COMIC BOOK LAYOUT PAGE

NOTES   PAGE #

NOTES   PAGE #

NOTES   PAGE #

NOTES   PAGE #

COMIC BOOK LAYOUT PAGE

NOTES   PAGE #

NOTES   PAGE #

NOTES   PAGE #

NOTES   PAGE #

COMIC BOOK LAYOUT PAGE

NOTES   PAGE #

NOTES   PAGE #

TITLE:

NOTES   PAGE #

NOTES   PAGE #

COMIC BOOK LAYOUT PAGE

NOTES   PAGE #

NOTES   PAGE #

TITLE:

NOTES

PAGE #

_____
_____
_____
_____
_____
_____
_____
_____
_____
_____
_____
_____
_____
_____
_____

NOTES

PAGE #

_____
_____
_____
_____
_____
_____
_____
_____
_____
_____
_____
_____
_____
_____
_____

COMIC BOOK LAYOUT PAGE

NOTES   PAGE #

NOTES   PAGE #

NOTES   PAGE #

NOTES   PAGE #

COMIC BOOK LAYOUT PAGE

NOTES   PAGE #

NOTES   PAGE #

NOTES   PAGE #

NOTES   PAGE #

COMIC BOOK LAYOUT PAGE

NOTES   PAGE #

NOTES   PAGE #

NOTES   PAGE #

NOTES   PAGE #

COMIC BOOK LAYOUT PAGE

NOTES   PAGE #

NOTES   PAGE #

FINAL ART PAGES

USE THESE PAGES TO DRAW YOUR FINAL COMICS!

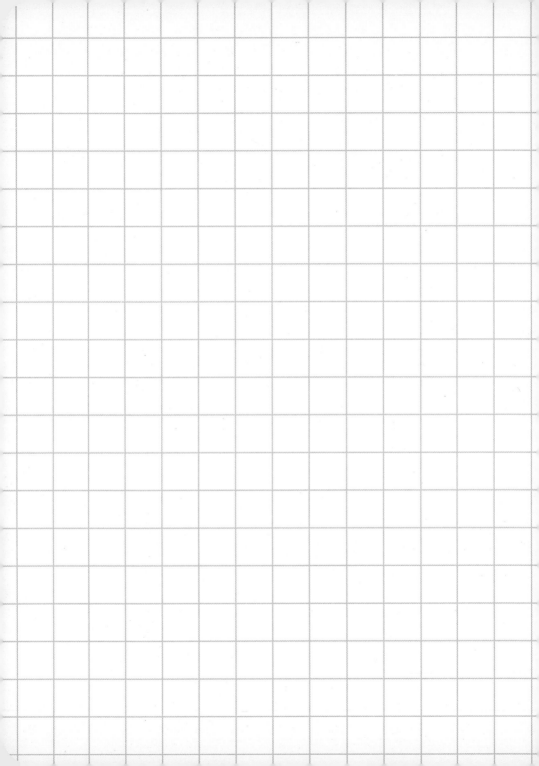